Rest in the Shadow

A Study of Psalm 91

JOHN C. SORRELL

WESTBOW·
PRESS
A DIVISION OF THOMAS NELSON
& ZONDERVAN

Scripture taken from the New King James Version. Copyright 1979, 1980, 1982 by Thomas Nelson, inc. Used by permission. All rights reserved.

Scripture quotations taken from the Holy Bible, New Living Translation, copyright 1996, 2004. Used by permission of Tyndale House Publishers, Inc., Wheaton, Illinois 60189. All rights reserved.

Scriptures taken from the Holy Bible, New International Version®, NIV®. Copyright © 1973, 1978, 1984, 2011 by Biblica, Inc.™ Used by permission of Zondervan. All rights reserved worldwide. www.zondervan.com The "NIV" and "New International Version" are trademarks registered in the United States Patent and Trademark Office by Biblica, Inc.™ All rights reserved.

Scripture quotations taken from the New American Standard Bible®, Copyright © 1960, 1962, 1963, 1968, 1971, 1972, 1973, 1975, 1977, 1995 by The Lockman Foundation. Used by permission." (www.Lockman.org)

Scripture taken from the Holman Christian Standard Bible ® Copyright © 2003, 2002, 2000, 1999 by Holman Bible Publishers. All rights reserved.

Scripture taken from The Living Bible copyright © 1971 by Tyndale House Foundation. Used by permission of Tyndale House Publishers Inc., Carol Stream, Illinois 60188. All rights reserved. The Living Bible, TLB, and the The Living Bible logo are registered trademarks of Tyndale House Publishers.

WestBow Press books may be ordered through booksellers or by contacting:

WestBow Press
A Division of Thomas Nelson & Zondervan
1663 Liberty Drive
Bloomington, IN 47403
www.westbowpress.com
1 (866) 928-1240

ISBN: 978-1-4908-8845-3 (sc)
ISBN: 978-1-4908-8846-0 (hc)
ISBN: 978-1-4908-8847-7 (e)

Print information available on the last page.

WestBow Press rev. date: 07/29/2015

CONTENTS

PROLOGUE

Freshly delivered from slavery at the hands of an unjust pharaoh the Hebrew nation began its 40 year pilgrimage across the Sinai wilderness. Early on in the wandering process, God gave Moses some very explicit architectural plans from which to build the portable tabernacle. It is in this tabernacle where His glory would fill the dwelling in the form of a cloud by day and a fire by night. "Then the cloud covered the tabernacle of meeting, and the glory of the Lord filled the tabernacle." [Exodus 40:34 NKJV]

Step forward five hundred years and we see the construction of the permanent temple, where once again God gave detailed and deliberate directions for this exquisite temple which would become His new dwelling. "When the children of Israel saw how the fire came down, and saw how the glory of the Lord filled the temple, they bowed their faces to the ground on the pavement, and worshiped and praised the Lord, saying:

> 'For He is good, for His mercy endures forever.'"
> [2 Chronicles 7:3 NKJV]

Now move forward in scripture to Psalm 91 where God identifies yet another dwelling place. This fortress includes ample space for others to join Him. Included for the dweller is the provision of both **refuge** and **rest**. The visual of God's glory and presence is manifest in a new way in this psalm. His shadow and His wings now replace the cloud of His presence.

For us to assume that the maker of the universe would need a place to dwell would be an unfounded presumption, and to further assume that He would need us to provide it for Him would be a stretch. It is for our sakes and benefit that God would designate a particular location in which He would dwell.

It is in this shelter and place of refuge where we will spend our time reflecting on the joy of living in God's very presence. It is my prayer that our study will aid us in understanding the character of a protector God who calls His children to join Him in this fortress. We will address the fundamental issue of living in God's presence and the benefits afforded to the one who will "Rest in the Shadow."

INTRODUCTION

I love the mountains! The Rockies, the Blue Ridge, the Ozarks where I was born, the Alps, the Adirondacks, the Andes, and the Scottish Highlands have all enchanted me.

My favorite time of day is the half-light of the early morning when long shadows slide down the granite and tree strewn face of these edifices. It is a time of awakening to soft pastels that are fleeting in this post-dawn moment.

After a summer's day has warmed the air, these same shadows reappear to begin calming and cooling the evening to come. These are the peaceful moments, both restful and reflective. This is a place and time where the hands on the clock do not seem to progress, a "rest in the shadow" moment in time.

It is God's plan that we should experience such times in our hurried lives. It is His desire that we gather in the shelter of His dwelling to find rest in His shadow.

As I conclude this introduction, allow me to retrace my steps to the mountains I love with a quote from the Psalm of Moses. "Before the mountains were born, before you gave birth to the

earth and the world, from beginning to end, you are God."
[Psalm 90:2 NLT]

From beginning to end, you are God...

Psalm 91

1 He who dwells in the shelter of the Most High
will rest in the shadow of the Almighty.
2 I will say of the LORD, "He is my refuge and
my fortress, my God, in whom I trust."
3 Surely he will save you from the fowler's
snare and from the deadly pestilence.
4 He will cover you with his feathers, and under his wings you
will find refuge; his faithfulness will be your shield and rampart.
5 You will not fear the terror of night,
nor the arrow that flies by day,
6 nor the pestilence that stalks in the darkness,
nor the plague that destroys at midday.
7 A thousand may fall at your side, ten thousand at
your right hand, but it will not come near you.
8 You will only observe with your eyes and
see the punishment of the wicked.
9 If you make the Most High your dwelling--
even the LORD, who is my refuge—
10 then no harm will befall you, no
disaster will come near your tent.
11 For he will command his angels concerning
you to guard you in all your ways;
12 they will lift you up in their hands, so that you
will not strike your foot against a stone.
13 You will tread upon the lion and the cobra; you
will trample the great lion and the serpent.
14 "Because he loves me," says the LORD, "I will rescue
him; I will protect him, for he acknowledges my name.
15 He will call upon me, and I will answer him; I will be
with him in trouble, I will deliver him and honor him.
16 With long life will I satisfy him and show him my salvation."

NIV 1984

CHAPTER 1

* If you're using <u>Rest in the Shadow</u> as a small group Bible study, see note at beginning of 'Chapter One Bible Study Questions.'

Psalm 91, whose author is unknown, was written for encouragement and personal application. Through the centuries many have literally carried this psalm in their pockets and in their hearts as they have left for battle or left their mother countries to go to foreign shores.

"He who dwells in the shelter of the Most High, will rest in the shadow of the Almighty. I will say of the Lord, 'He is my refuge and my fortress my God in whom I trust.'" vs. 1 and 2

The descriptive nature of this psalm presents God as a competent protector whose sovereign covering over His children keeps them safe from possible intruders who may attempt to lay siege to this fortress. These verses are personalized by the use of the first person pronouns *I* and *my*. It is written so that we may also personalize this text in application to our lives which will identify ownership - not that we have ownership but that we are owned. We have been bought with a price as one ransomed to be set free.

I have always pictured this place of safety as a mountain fortress, perhaps because of Psalm 121:1, "I will lift my eyes to the mountains; from whence shall my help come? My help comes from the Lord, who made heaven and earth." [NAS] This mountain shelter makes us think of Moses who met with God on Mount Sinai. God spoke to Moses, "So it shall be, while My glory passes by, that I will put you in the cleft of the rock, and will cover you with my hand while I pass by." [Exodus 33:22 NKJV] King David also found safety in the mountain cave. "David therefore departed from there and escaped to the cave of Adullam." [I Samuel 22:1] The secret place of the caves or the clefts of the mountain walls are only temporary places of safety. God's gift is long-term rest and refuge in His place of dwelling.

*

The two names for God in verse one would help to validate this visual. The Hebrew translation, El-Elyon, means "the Most High God," which stresses His sovereignty and strength. El-Shaddai, also found in verse one, is usually translated into English as "God Almighty," but is sometimes identified as "the God of the mountains." The visual of this mountain fortress may lead to a presumption that God is far away and unreachable. That is not the picture painted by the writer of this psalm, as we will see in the verses to come.

"Rest in the Shadow" is a beautiful visual of God's provision of comfort for His child who abides in His presence. A young lady once told me of growing up in New Mexico where the summer sun would scorch the sands that made up her playground. To escape the burning sand she found refuge for her bare feet in the shade of an occasional tree. So, she would run from tree to tree in order to rest in the shadow seemingly cast for her personal comfort and pleasure. The shadow cooled the sand, and resting in the shade of the tree brought relief to her small feet.

The promises found in this psalm are available to every believer but are not enjoyed by all who call themselves His children, for what is described through the entirety of this psalm is only for those who choose an intimate relationship with "the Almighty." All who are children of God, adopted into His family, have the opportunity for this fellowship and protection, and though we are heirs to all the riches God has available and has supplied for us, we do not partake in this wonderful inheritance. All of us do not "dwell in the shelter."

Charles Haddon Spurgeon, the great English preacher of the nineteenth century, said, "They run to it at times, and enjoy occasional approaches, but they do not habitually reside in the mysterious presence." [C.H. Spurgeon, *The Treasury of David*, Volume 2, (Peabody, MA: Hendrickson Publishers), 88]

*

The key in understanding the depth of verse one in Psalm 91 is found in the word *dwell*. Perhaps the exchange of the words *reside, live or abide* for the word dwell will give us a better perspective as we look at the invitation offered by a loving Father.

Let us begin here.

As a child I always felt happy and safe when spending the night at my grandmother's house. I do not know that I could put my finger on the reason, but there was much security in being in her home. There were some things I was sure of when visiting that mountain home in Arkansas, such as a soft, warm bed where a night's sleep went uninterrupted until morning, and a hot breakfast that only Grandma could make. The smells from the humble kitchen of hot biscuits and bacon would intrude on my comfortable resting place. The sense of unconditional love and familiar laughter was my encouragement to run and place my small arms around her aproned waist.

Joel 3:16b says, "But the Lord will be a shelter for His people."

The presence of God brings security, just as the absence of His presence brings anxious and often fearful thoughts. Psalm 121:3 reads, "He will not allow your foot to slip; He who keeps you will not slumber. 4. Behold, He who keeps Israel will neither slumber nor sleep. 5. The Lord is your keeper; The Lord is your shade on your right hand. 6. The sun will not smite you by day, nor the moon by night. 7. The Lord will protect you from all evil; He will keep your soul. 8. The Lord will guard your going out or your coming in from this time forth and forever."

This sister psalm identifies the protection offered by God to those who belong to Him. The significance of the word "shade" in verse 5 infers comfort as does the word "shadow" in Psalm 91:2. Let me say here that God is not just providing protection for our safety; He is our protection, He is our rest and He is our peace. Protection, rest and peace are located in God Himself. It is our God who is with us and our Christ who is in us who provide such pleasures.

The following is a quote from Mary Duncan found in the text of her 1867 writing, *Under the Shadow.*

> "He that dwelleth in the secret place of the Most High." What intimate and unrestrained communion does this describe! – the Christian in everything making known his heart, with its needs and wishes, its thoughts and feelings, its doubts and anxieties, its sorrows and its joys, to God, as to a loving, perfect friend. And all is not on one side. This Almighty Friend has admitted His chosen one to His secret place. It is almost too wonderful to be true. It is almost too presumptuous a thought for such creatures as we to entertain. But He himself permits it, desires it, and teaches us to realize that it is communion to which He calls us. "The secret of the Lord is with them that fear Him." And what is the secret? It is that in God which the world neither knows, nor sees, nor cares to enjoy. It is His mind revealed to those that love Him, His plans and ways and thoughts open to them. Yea, and things hid from angels are manifest to the least of His friends, (I Peter 1:12). He wishes us to know Him, and by His Word and by His Spirit He puts Himself before us. Ah! It is not His fault if we do not know Him. It is our carelessness. [C.H. Spurgeon,

The Treasury of David, Volume 2, (Peabody, MA: Hendrickson Publishers), 95]

It is in this "shelter" or "secret place" where His Shekinah glory lights up the entire room to dispel the darkness that hides the frightening unknowns.

It is the fear of the unknowns which often cripples us and causes retreat to the safety of our small candle lit corner. God has prepared a light-filled mansion that uncovers every possible obstacle or obstruction which was previously hidden in the dark. The fearful unknowns appear larger and more ominous than they do in the light.

*

James 4:2, "The reason you don't have what you want is that you don't ask God for it."

Hebrews 4:16 tells us that as His children we can "come boldly before the throne of God."

A.W. Tozer wrote, "When our requests are such as honor God we may ask as largely as we will. The more daring the request, the more glory accrues to God when the answer comes." [A. W. Tozer, *My Daily Pursuit,* James L. Snyder editor (Regal Publishers, 2013)]

Ask largely. Use God-honoring requests. And listen quietly, safe and secure in His dwelling.

"How firm a foundation, ye saints of the Lord,
Is laid for your faith in His excellent Word!
What more can He say than to you He hath said
to you who for refuge to Jesus have fled."

["How Firm a Foundation," Rippon's *Selections of Hymns*, 1787]

Martin Luther's great Reformation hymn gives us insight into why we have need of this fortress.

A mighty fortress is our God, A bulwark never failing.
Our helper He amid the flood of mortal ills prevailing.
For still our ancient foe doth seek to work us woe,
his craft and power are great and armed with cruel hate,
on earth is not his equal.

Did we in our own strength confide, Our striving
would be losing.
Were not the right man on our side a man of God's
on choosing.
Dost ask who that may be? Christ Jesus it is He
Lord Sabaoth His name, from age to age the same,
and He must win the battle.

[Martin Luther; translated by Frederick H. Hedge, "A Mighty Fortress Is Our God"]

סֶלָה

Selah – Chapter One

We are dwellers not because we have earned the right to be dwellers, but because we have been invited to rest here. No merit of good works or good attitude opens this door for us.

We who once were unclean, full of sin and self-love have been offered an interlude and respite. Though knowledgeable of our former condition, both fearful and full of repute, we now have been given an opportunity to step into this mountain refuge and there abide in His shadow as sons, daughters and heirs. He is now our provision.

So we join the grand chorus of the ages singing, "Kyrie eleison, Emmanuel, God is with us." Soaring phrases reflect off the fortress walls to be heard a millennia later by new dwellers, for this door is never closed to those who are called by His name.

*Selah is a Hebrew musical term implying stop and listen. The Amplified Bible published jointly by The Zondervan Corporation and The Lockman Foundation in 1965 states, concerning the word selah; "pause and calmly think about that" and "pause and weigh the meaning."

Therefore I conclude each chapter with a Selah, suggesting, take a moment and reflect.

CHAPTER 2

*

"Surely He will save you from the fowler's snare and from the deadly pestilence. He will cover you with His feathers, and under His wings you will find refuge; His faithfulness will be your shield and your rampart." vs. 3 and 4

The psalmist uses repetition with the words He, He, His, His and His, confirming over and over in these first verses that it is God Himself who will do the work. This of course takes us out of the picture as having accomplished anything by our own will or merit. We sit somewhat as observers to all that God will do on our behalf.

In verse three we have our first introduction as to the schemes of the enemy with the phrase "the fowler's snare." Old and New Testament scriptures often remind us of the battle waged for the souls of man. Ephesians 6 is a New Testament description of our battle wear and protective armor. Psalm 91 intimates and explains that the Most High is our protection.

Now back to verse three and the introductory word "save." The Hebrew word is "nasal," which literally means "to be snatched away from, or rescued from." The word was used countless times by David when he asked God to "save" him from his enemies. The Hebrew word appears many times throughout the Psalms with the theme of deliverance.

The "fowler's snare" is a camouflaged trap, set in a specific location, at a specific time to capture the fowl. Like any other snare, this one is strategic in its location in relation to the proximity of the prey. It is placed in the path where the fowl will travel or where the fowl will gather to feed. The phrase "He will save you" is the visual of the Father releasing the prisoner from the enemy's trap. A foolish bird can be easily lured in by attractive bait set by a cunning foe. We also can be attracted to a multitude of baits that ultimately will bring about our capture and demise. Wisdom in identifying the bait as dangerous, although alluring, will keep us from being snared.

*

I am an avid fly fisherman, having been attracted to the sport by the beauty of the location and the art of seducing the fish to feed on a hand-tied bait. As a fly fisherman my objective is to fool the fish with an artificial fly that looks like the real thing. The trout will not go after just any fly that floats in his feeding path. The trout is selective in what he will strike. First, it has to be something he is attracted to at that moment and looks like the food source that is available in season. Many times I have stood knee deep in a stream with a trout clearly waiting near a small boulder to feed off the next tempting morsel. Time after time the trout will ignore my fly or swim near and reject it. Sometimes the trout is wise to the fake because he has been caught before.

Have there been traps set for you by the enemy, camouflaged and covered with leaves and dust ready to snare you? Some traps are set with very intriguing bait which would be difficult to reject especially when floated in front of your face again and again. It is the Holy Spirit who works in us to do the will of the Father that prompts us to recognize the trap that has been laid by the enemy. It is often that God's deliverance takes place before we have been snared.

*

"From the deadly pestilence," is identified as the next attack of the enemy. It is this section of the psalm that causes some commentators to think that Psalm 91 was written by Moses. Remember how God delivered the children of Israel from the deadly pestilence that struck down Pharaoh's kingdom?

"If all the saints are not so sheltered it is because they have not all such a close abiding with God, and consequently not such confidence in the promise." [Spurgeon, *The Treasury of David*, 90]

There is no recourse from the "noisome pestilence," it comes in when we are unaware, and suddenly it is too late. So it remains; it is God who watches over us, "the one who does not sleep nor slumber." We will never know this side of heaven why we have been kept from infectious disease or from a catastrophic event. How many times has God taken us out of harm's way?

Vs. 4 "He will cover you with His feathers and under His wings you will find refuge." Notice again the repetition of *He* and *His*. He is constantly drawing us to Himself so that we might be dependent on Him, realizing that in our own strength we will surely fail. **His** feathers, **His** wings, and the provision of **His** refuge.

What a beautiful word picture to someone who spent many years on the farm - the visual of a mother hen sitting on the ground with her feathers all fluffed out, when suddenly you see a little head pop out from beneath the feathers, followed by another and then another. When she stands there is a scattering of six, eight, or perhaps ten chicks who are looking for something to eat or simply to investigate their surroundings. Just as quickly, the mother hen will make a single chirp and every chick retreats to be covered once again by her feathers as she raises her wings to provide protection.

Ruth 2:12, "...the God of Israel, under whose wings you have come to seek refuge."

The picture here is of great tenderness and care. The mother hen is keeping the chicks secret, protected and comfortable. Have you ever slept under a down-filled comforter in the middle of January? The comforter provides warmth for the entire night's sleep. The visual painted by the psalmist is of confident security and comfort.

*

David wrote when fleeing from Saul to the protection of the cave; "Be merciful to me, O God, be merciful to me! For my soul trusts in You: And in the shadow of Your wings I will make my refuge, until the calamities have passed by." Psalm 57:1

Psalm 91:4b "His faithfulness will be our shield and our rampart."

It is His faithfulness, not ours. His provision is not just armor, but double armor. He bears a shield and a coat of protective mail, or in another interpretation, a protective wall.

The shield would be equivalent to what we find in the warfare chapter in the New Testament. In the sixth chapter of Ephesians this shield is listed among the required armor. "Taking up the shield of faith, which will help you extinguish the fiery darts (flaming arrows) of the enemy."

Satan's darts and arrows are defended against through the effective use of the shield of faith. The tactics of the enemy seldom changes. The reason the tactics seldom change is because it continues to work. We fall for the timeless bait of lies that has attracted men and women through the ages.

"His faithfulness," better translated from the original language, is "His truth."

Truth brings victory because the battle we are fighting is against the lies perpetrated by the enemy. These lies are whispered in our ears by the enemy. We are reminded that he is "the father of lies" and these lies are "his native language." The exchange of the truth for lies allows strongholds to dominate our lives. When lies from the enemy are whispered in our ears and then validated by circumstance a stronghold can easily be established which may dominate our lives. Often the lies are whispered against us by those who set out to do the enemy's dirty work. More than once through many years of ministry I have heard these words come from a counselee; "It would have been better if I had never been born." When I ask why do you believe this lie? I hear the same phrase repeated, "That is what my father always told me." For years the counselee may have rejected these untruths until some situation or circumstance comes along and appears to validate that statement.

God remains our bastion of strength and security as Isaiah wrote "For You have been a strength to the poor, a strength to the needy in distress, a refuge from the storm, a shade from the heat; for the blast of the terrible ones is a storm against the wall." Isaiah 25:4

All of us desire to be secure and safe from anything that would be destructive to us physically, mentally or emotionally. The enemy's ploy is to find ways to get through or around the wall of deliverance made available by our Father Protector, by way of His faithfulness and truth.

*

סֶלָה

Selah – Chapter Two

Morning creeps up on you in the mountains, like the music of dawn's first bird, distant and soothing as a familiar hymn. The light first catches the highest peaks and walks down its face until the valley is bathed in gold.

The lyric voice of the stream that rocked you to sleep in the night almost disappears with the daylight. The stream however is never really silent. It calls you throughout the day. Her voice is soft and romantic, yet loud enough to be heard weeks later when the world rushes in with a suffocating urgency.

My visits to these snowcapped edifices are brief but linger for a lifetime when recaptured and painted with memory's brush.

CHAPTER 3

"You will not fear the terror of night, nor the arrow that flies by day, nor the pestilence that stalks in the darkness, nor the plague that destroys at midday. A thousand may fall at your side, ten thousand at your right hand, but it will not come near you. You will only observe with your eyes and see the punishment of the wicked." v. 5-8

*

Fear is controlling. Fear is a bully who backs you into a corner to defeat your will and bring you into servitude. Fear causes us to look over our shoulder at every turn in order to make us anxious and ready to flee. It is the inherent response of a horse called the flight response, which originates deep within the DNA as a mode of protection. Spending much of my life around horses I saw firsthand how quickly they can be calmly grazing in the pasture and then in the next moment bolt in a full run at the slightest of movements.

Satan is a bully, and as a bully his intention is to strike his prey with fear. His desire and objective is to intimidate so he can control you. Fretful, anxious and fearful are all part of his personal infliction vocabulary used against those who do not "take refuge" in the dwelling of the Most High. Paul wrote to Timothy, "For God has not given us a spirit of fearfulness, but one of power, love and sound judgment." [I Timothy 1:7 HCSB]

Vs. 5 "You will not fear." This is a statement of promise to the one who "rests in the shadow."

God's desire for His children is to experience peace and joy in whatever circumstance they find themselves. Philippians 4:11 says, "Not that I speak in regard to need, for I have learned in whatever state I am in, to be content." Much can be written here in the context of fear and Satan's use of fear to cause dysfunction in the life of the believer. We are overcomers of fear because of the "power that works within us."

Verse 5 introduces us to "the terror of night." Why does it come? What can be done about this terror when it comes? One of the most interesting things about this section of Psalm 91 is that it holds several elements of potential fear, all of which we can do little or nothing about.

One thing we can purposely do is recognize the source. Who has not been awakened by an unexplained terror or fear in the middle of a night's sleep? A heart-pounding, sheet-tossed moment of unexplained fear or terror can intrude on an otherwise uneventful night's rest. When we recognize the source then we can hold up the shield of faith which "extinguishes the arrows of the enemy."

I find it also helps to pray a bedtime prayer like this. "Lord Jesus, I thank You that You are watching over me throughout this night. I ask that Your blood be a hedge around my body, soul, spirit and mind. Do not allow anything to intrude on my sleep that doesn't first come by the way of the cross and through the blood of Jesus. Protect me by Your love and grace throughout the dark hours of the night. I thank You for this in Jesus' name."

Psalm 31: 19-20, "How great is Thy goodness, which Thou hast stored up for those that fear Thee, which Thou hast wrought for those who take refuge in Thee, before the sons of men! Thou dost hide them in the secret place of Thy presence from the conspiracies of man; Thou dost keep them secretly in a shelter from the strife of tongues."

"Tongues" may also translate lies or accusations. These lies and accusations always originate from a singular source which is the enemy, or as John in his gospel identified, "the ruler of this world." Who is the target of these accusations and lies? We are. They are directed at us in order to stifle our productivity in being a light to a world that lives in darkness.

✳

Vs. 5b "Nor the arrow that flies by day." Remember back in verse 4 where God says "My truth will be your shield?" The lies will be defended against by God's truth, His "faithfulness." In our own strength, we are not able to defend ourselves against the terrors, arrows, pestilences and plagues. However, so many of us, even as God's adopted children, attempt to fight all of these in our strength. We use popular feel good strategies or pop psychology in hopes that we will feel better about ourselves or develop a way to live more comfortably in this relentless bombardment from hell.

Charles Spurgeon said of this pestilence that walks in the darkness, "It is shrouded in mystery as to its cause and cure; it marches on unseen of men, slaying with hidden weapons like an enemy stabbing in the dark; yet those who dwell in God are not afraid of it." [*The Treasury of David*, 91]

The pestilence, as well as the plague, sneaks into men's houses unannounced and does it mortal damage, exiting by the rear door to seek out another unsuspecting victim.

Though pestilence may enter by way of the darkness, the child of God has the privilege of living in full light. "For you were once darkness, but now [you are] full light in the Lord. Walk as children of light for the fruit of the light [results] in all goodness, righteousness and truth discerning what is pleasing to the Lord. Don't participate in the fruitless works of darkness, but instead, expose them. For it is shameful even to mention what is done by them in secret. Everything exposed by the light is made clear, for what makes everything clear is light." Ephesians 5:8-14a

*

How many times throughout history has God sent His messenger with the opening phrase "do not be afraid?" Only God would introduce His message with the opening statement "do not be afraid." The angel Gabriel as God's messenger said to Zacharias, "Do not be afraid, Zacharias, for your prayer is heard." Again the angel Gabriel spoke these words to Mary, "Do not be afraid, for you have found favor with God." Again concerning the announcement of Christ's birth the angel spoke these same words to the shepherds, "Do not be afraid, for behold, I bring you good tidings of great joy which will be to all people." God not only brings safety to His children, He instills a personal peace and calm.

Vs. 7 "A thousand may fall at your side, ten thousand at your right hand, but it will not come near you."

Matthew Henry, though deceased for three centuries, gave us these wise words, "The sprinkling of blood secured the first born of Israel when thousands fell. Nay, it is promised to God's people that they shall have the satisfaction of seeing, not only God's promises fulfilled to them, but His threatening fulfilled upon those that hate them." [*Matthew Henry's Commentary*, Volume 3, (Peabody: Hendrickson Publishers, 1991), 481]

Verses 7 and 8 read like a battle scene as being described from a distant hillside. This description may have a direct relationship to the covenant promises God made to Israel. The Israelites saw firsthand the dead of the first born and the Egyptian army engulfed by the Red Sea. Yet no harm came to the people of Israel. God's angel went before them to prepare the way. God provided a cloud by day and a fire by night, manna and quail in the wilderness and water from the rock.

What is the terror that strikes you in the night, or what arrow has been aimed directly at you? What pestilence or plague is at your doorstep this day? Our present-day list of pestilences and plagues could be lengthy and include things like loss of job, divorce, or a prodigal child. God is still making available His shelter as a refuge and a fortress for those who will trust in Him. This does not mean there will be no suffering, pestilence, trouble... It does mean that during suffering, pestilence, and troubles, "I will be with him," and "I will never leave you nor forsake you."

*

Without the experience of crisis, we are often only speaking from theory, though the theory may be correct. Ministry occurs through the use of biblical truth and validated through the experience of crisis and tragedy as exampled by Simon Peter. Here is the conversation between Jesus and Peter. "Simon, Simon! Satan has asked to have you, to sift you like wheat, but I have prayed on your behalf so that you will not surely fail. When it is over you will return to me and be able to strengthen the brethren."

Peter was familiar with the ploys of the enemy. He sometimes became an easy target due to his robust and aggressive personality, and at least on this one occasion Satan was allowed to "have" him.

When we are allowed to go through temptation there is always a purpose and in Simon Peter's case it was to "strengthen the brethren."

The reality of Peter's trial was fleshed out in scripture decades later when he wrote these words, "Be sober, be vigilant; because your adversary the devil walks about like a roaring lion seeking whom he may devour. Resist him, steadfast in the faith, knowing that the same sufferings are experienced by your brotherhood in the world."

We will suffer anguish, trauma, and strife in our walk with Christ. Jesus told his disciples, "You will suffer persecution because of me." It is often after going through a very difficult season of life that ministry opportunity begins. We can relate to and begin to live out the statement Jesus spoke to Peter, "When it is all over ... you will be able to strengthen the brethren."

*

Selah – Chapter Three

As I awake to Your glories, Your praise lies softly on my tongue, and my heart sings a glad song. The song of deliverance and peace comes from You the Giver of Life who bore my sorrow and shame. Therefore on the day I return to dust to be blown into field and stream Your name will be fresh on my lips.

Take my fear and my anxious thoughts to a foreign destination. Far from me let them reside alone in a desolate place never to be retrieved. With Your hand lift my face and turn my eyes once again to Your greatness.

You alone can take my iniquities to dismiss them to the far reaches of the universe. You cast the shadow of Your unseen face upon the waters and land, dispersing grace to all who will receive. Therefore, I will sing the angels song, "Holy, holy, holy is the Lord God Almighty. The whole earth is filled with Your glory."

CHAPTER 4

*

"You will only observe with your eyes and see the punishment of the wicked. If you make the Most High your dwelling- even the Lord, who is my refuge- then no harm will befall you, no disaster will come near your tent." vs. 8-10

To emphasize an important point in your message, it is often good to use a poignant story you've read or heard from a popular speaker or writer. To bring emphasis to these two verses of scripture, I will use my own story.

In the late 1980's, when Eastern Europe was still under the thumb of the Soviet Union, I traveled with a small group of men to do ministry in Poland and in the Soviet Republic of Belarus. Our first several days were spent in Warsaw, Poland where we lived in seminary housing while participating in ministry and preparing for our trip to Minsk, Belarus. Since it was the dead of winter, snow covered the ground where it had been shoveled from sidewalks and streets. Before leaving Warsaw, we were asked by the local church if we would carry Russian language Bibles with us to give to the church in Minsk. We agreed and filled suitcases and overcoat pockets with these Russian language Bibles. Moving to our next short term destination, we arrived by train in the town of Bialystok which sat on the western border of this Soviet occupied country. Bialystok is a beautifully forested Polish city whose population is second only to Warsaw. Prior to World War II, it was a predominately Jewish city; however, all remnants of the Jewish population no longer exist except in memory. The local synagogue has been kept as a shrine but no longer functions as a place of worship. Our time was to be brief since we were anxious to experience our first trip into Cold War era USSR.

After boarding our train and moving into our very small sleeper car we traveled only a few miles before the train stopped and stood still for the next several hours while all the wheels on the train were exchanged in order to accommodate a different width track. Because of Stalin's paranoia, he dictated that all the tracks leading into Russia would be a different width from those in Western Europe. This would prevent Russia from being invaded by rail from the west. It was during this point in my trip that I experienced the intimidation of Russian soldiers as they intruded into our car with rifles and machine guns in hand. They asked for our passports, which they quickly gathered, and exited our sleeper car. Sometime later they reentered with more soldiers and began to systematically go through our suitcases and overcoats. As they poured over all the contents of our suitcases, it was as if they never saw the dozens and dozens of Bibles. It happened again and again as they opened suitcase after suitcase and scavenged the pockets of our heavy overcoats. No questions were asked as to why we were carrying so many Russian language Bibles. These Bibles were considered contraband and were illegal to bring into the country during this cold war period of history. They exited our car within about half an hour and within another hour we were on our way east toward our snow covered destination. To me this was a living demonstration of "But, it will not harm you."

This final phrase of verse 7 "**But,** it will not harm you," is a reminder of the blood painted over the door posts protecting the first born Hebrew children during final days of enslavement in Egypt just as God had directed and promised Moses. This sprinkling of blood caused the death angel to pass over this place of residence. The sprinkling of blood is also a reminder of what God did for us by way of the cross and the blood that was shed by Christ. The shedding of blood by the unblemished sacrificial lamb forces death and hell to pass over the believer with the words "O Death where is your victory, O Grave, where is your sting?" [I Corinthians 15:55]

*

Exodus 12: 13, "And the blood shall be a sign for you on the houses where you live; and when I see the blood I will pass over you, and no plague will befall you to destroy you when I strike the land of Egypt."

It is this section of the Psalm where God begins to make it personal. He turns the pronoun from Himself in verses 1-6 and redirects the language for the sake of His children.

In verses 7 through 10, the words and phrases you and your redirect the narrative back to the dweller, which identifies the recipient of His love and protection.

He is protecting us from **harm**. The Hebrew word for harm is **ra,** an adjective meaning "that which is bad, evil, wicked, or corrupt." Many places in the Old Testament **ra,** is translated "evil." Examples can be found in multiple Old Testament texts such as evil words (Prov. 15:26), evil thoughts (Gen. 6:5) and evil actions (Prov. 2:14, Exodus 5:22-23). Therefore, no evil will come against you, or, if we hear God's voice in this statement He is saying, "I will not allow you to be the target of evil."

In verse 8 we become observers, as were the children of Israel. "But Moses said to the people, 'Do not fear! Stand by and see the salvation of the Lord which He will accomplish for you today; for the Egyptians whom you have seen today, you will never see them again **forever.**'" As observers we are watching our enemy from a distance where we do not see firsthand the ravages of war or the things of horror that insight fear and make even the bravest soldier desire a place of hiding and safety.

Proverbs 29:25, "The fear of man brings a snare, but whoever trusts in the Lord shall be safe."

*

God has made a way of escape for His children by providing security in Himself. It is a natural response to be fearful when tragedy is striking all around us and it is easy to become overwhelmed. We can also be overly preoccupied, anxious, and fretful because of the situations of loved ones. As adults we will often find ourselves in situations affecting our children, grandchildren, parents and friends. These times of crisis can be all too consuming. In taking on the burden of those we love, the element of fear or evil will often be too heavy to carry around in our busy lives. Resting in the promise of "no harm will befall you, no disaster will come near your tent," can bring relief when shouldering such a weight.

However, God is not the god of the Ancient Greek play who intrudes to change the outcome of the script so the good guy wins. He is not the hero of the silent movie who unties the damsel from the train tracks at the last minute. Yet we have through the ages used Jehovah God as if He is obligated to swoop in and save us from whatever calamity may be occurring on that particular day. We do have the joyous privilege during these difficult times to make a choice. We can run to the shelter He has provided or give up and say, "There is nothing that can be done."

The enemy can appear as a kind, child loving, gracious and caring person. He or she can wear a mask that disguises the real evil intent of the heart and actions. John Gotti, the famed mob boss, was an example of such a schizophrenic personality. Convicted of murder, fraud, money laundering and attempt to commit murder would normally identify you as one bad dude. However, while in prison he wrote a tender children's book.

Good Housekeeping magazine published an article in 1938 about Adolph Hitler and his love for the arts and music. The article spoke of times when he would bring children into his modest estate where they would perform skits and sing songs to his delight. He would eat vegetarian meals; and though he provided alcoholic drinks to his guests along with cigarettes and cigars, he did not drink or smoke. This persona was used to hide the real Adolph Hitler who oversaw the murder of millions of Jews, gypsies, Poles and others.

I use both of these examples to identify the danger posed by the enemy who often camouflages his intent and sneaks into our lives in disguise. If we snuggle up close to the Father, we will have protection from the fraudulent enemies who sneak into our lives to bring curses rather than blessing.

Now the ball is placed in our court with the words "if you." You must exert your will and make the choice. "If **you** make the Most High your dwelling- even the Lord, who is my refuge-then no harm will befall **you,** no disaster will come near **your** tent." You are given the opportunity to respond out of obedience to the invitation of the Father.

*

If the Lord is truly our habitation, then there should be no other place of residence for His children. However, we often return to wander the dark streets of our past. On one hand God protects us **from dangers** and again protects us **in dangers**; however, there are times when He protects us **by dangers**. A biblical example of this is given by Charles Haddon Spurgeon in his exposition of the ninety-first psalm. Let me paraphrase this great English preacher. Jonah was swallowed by a whale and by that danger was kept alive. Joseph was thrown into a pit, afterwards sold to Egyptian slave traders, and by these dangers was not only kept alive but thrived. Esther was kept alive with the words, "if I perish, I perish."

By her obedience she became God's instrument to preserve His covenant promise to Abraham.

Is it possible you have gone through some tragedy, trial, persecution or deep trouble in order that you may come out on the other side to find yourself in the middle of God's plan and blessing? In reviewing this list of evils written in verses five and six (the terror, the arrow, the pestilence and the plague), I am reminded that God does not keep us from such evils, rather, He keeps us from the fear of evil.

*

Selah – Chapter Four

I look at the dry dirt beneath my feet and wonder, will it ever rain again? The wind picks up pieces of soil, sand and debris from what should be a lush green pasture and lifts them to rest in distant places. Is this the condition of my soul this day? Dry, to be dispersed on a neighbor's property only to be retrieved by the next breath of wind and redistributed to one more place of solitude.

No! For there was One, not as a martyr but as a servant, who took all my guilt, shame, pain, and regret to carry them with bent back to a place I will never have to go.

Willfully He chose to fulfill a plan made before time and lived out as if there had been years of dress rehearsals so that He who knew no sin might become sin for us. It was enough. Enough that in times of drought, when blown by a relentless wind, we can find a place of rest and solitude. Yet never alone.

> "What can wash away my sin? Nothing but the blood of Jesus.
> What can make me whole again? Nothing but the blood of Jesus.
> Oh, precious is the flow that makes me white as snow.
> No other fount I know. Nothing but the blood of Jesus." *
> *from the hymn "Nothing But the Blood" by Robert Lowry

CHAPTER 5

*

"For He will command His angels concerning you to guard you in all your ways; they will lift you up in their hands, so that you will not strike your foot against the stone." v. 11 and 12

This Old Testament passage of scripture is quoted in Matthew chapter 4. What is most interesting about this quote is the context of the conversation in this New Testament dialogue. This section of Psalm 91 was used by Satan during his second temptation of Christ.

Matthew 4:5, "Then the devil took him up into the holy city, set Him on the pinnacle of the temple, 6 and said to Him, "If You are the Son of God, throw Yourself down. For it is written: 'He shall give His angels change over you,' and 'in their hands they shall bear you up, lest you dash your foot against the stone.'" 7 Jesus said to him, "It is written again, 8 'you shall not tempt the Lord your God.'"

Let us take a respite here in the study of this psalm and look at God's provision and protection from another angle. As long as we abide in the dwelling and shelter of the Most High, there is protection. However, we will not always abide in this refuge and fortress where it is safe from the onslaught of the enemy. There will be times, many times, when God will allow a face to face confrontation with the enemy. It is always for our good and the benefit of others that God permits trials. One example of God's consent is identified in the temptations of Jesus as written in three of the Gospels. Matthew 4:1 reads, "Then Jesus was led by the Spirit into the wilderness to be tempted by the devil." Mark 1:12-13a contains a little stronger language, "Immediately the Spirit drove Him into the wilderness. And He was there in the wilderness forty days, tempted by Satan." Finally, Luke 4:1-2 states, "Then Jesus, being filled with the Holy Spirit, returned from the Jordan and was led by the Spirit into the wilderness, being tempted for forty days by the devil."

It is here, in the temptations of Christ, where we see exhibited the practice of a biblical principle which Paul was to identify concerning the "weapons of our warfare." Ephesians 6 identifies the whole armor of God, which is to be used in our defense against the enemy. The whole armor includes the belt of truth, the breastplate of righteousness, the gospel shoes, the shield of faith, the helmet of salvation and the sword of the spirit "which is the word of God."

Paul was definitively clear on who the enemy is. "For we do not wrestle against flesh and blood, but against principalities, against powers, against the rulers of the darkness of this age, against spiritual hosts of wickedness in the heavenly places." [Ephesians 6:12] Principalities, powers, rulers, and hosts are designated as those not of "flesh and blood." These layers of rankings identify spiritual beings and in particular the demons and their high level of structure in this Satan led empire. These levels of order were given to all the angels, both the holy angels who remained to obey God and the demon band, or one-third of the angel population who left to follow Satan. They are identified throughout God's word in no particular order as: archangel, cherubim, seraphim, principalities, powers, rulers and hosts. For our study we will not attempt to identify the assignments of each category of angel, rather to say these rankings exist.

Jesus answered the temptation of Satan by quoting Deuteronomy 6:16, therefore wielding the "sword of the Spirit, which is the word of God." In looking at the different pieces of the armor, you will quickly notice we have no offensive weapon other than "the sword of the Spirit," God's Word. The battle was obviously a very close hand to hand combat at this point. "Do not wrestle" is a picture of Satan's tactics. This is a close proximity battle that invades personal space, and pushes toward a quick response. This is always the tactic of a bully, and Satan is the master bully.

*

As we view the temptations of Christ through the lens of scripture, it is evident that the only thing Jesus said in response to the temptation placed in front of Him was brief and included an exact quote of Old Testament scripture. The writer of the little book of James used the phrase "resist the devil." Resist, or literally translated "stand against" or "stand in opposition to," leaves no out. The "sword of the Spirit, which is God's Word," is the only weapon made available to God's children. Ephesians

4:27 states "nor give place to the devil." Ephesians 6:11b gives substance to the action, "stand against the wiles of the devil." This is not a casual or passive stance because passivity leads to defeat, failure, humiliation and an ultimate retreat.

Peter was familiar with the ploys of the enemy. He sometimes became an easy target and at least on one occasion Satan was allowed to "have" him. The following conversation is found in Luke 22:31. "And the Lord said, 'Simon, Simon! Satan has asked for you, that he may sift you as wheat. But I have prayed for you, that your faith should not fail; and when you have returned to Me, strengthen the brethren.'" There are many implications to be found in these two verses of scripture, such as Christ's knowing what had happened in conversation between God the Father and Satan. The New American Standard translates verse 31 "Simon, Simon, behold, Satan has **demanded** permission to sift you like wheat." Another topic of study would be Jesus praying on Peter's behalf. "But I have prayed for you." For our use we will simply conclude that on occasion God will allow an attack or onslaught from the enemy. Permission is given always for a purpose, and in Simon Peter's case it was to "strengthen your brethren."

The reality of this experience will live itself out in Peter's life decades later when he penned these much quoted words as found in 1 Peter 4:8-9, "Be sober, be vigilant; because your adversary the devil walks about like a roaring lion, seeking whom he may devour. Resist him, steadfast in the faith, knowing that the same sufferings are experienced by your brotherhood in the world."

*

Job steps off the pages of biblical history with a key illustration. Let me paraphrase this encounter between God and Satan concerning Job.

As the angel hosts entered the presence of God they were accompanied by Satan. God questioned Satan as to where he had been which solicited this reply, "I've been watching all that is happening on the earth." God questioned, "Have you taken notice of my servant Job? He is the finest of them all, fears me and has kept the faith." Satan responded, "You have provided your protection for Job so why would he expect any harm to come to himself or his family. Let me have him and he will curse you to your face." God's response was, "Do as you please, but you must spare his life."

There is no indication in scripture that Job knew anything about what was taking place in the heavenly supernatural realm. There is no further indication that he ever knew. His life experience was catalogued as part of scripture, not for Job's sake nor for the sake of his family, but for those who came later. This story is for you and me today. Through the midst of Job's incomprehensible tragedies emerge two of the greatest statements of faith made by an Old Testament saint.

"Though He slays me, yet will I trust Him." [Job 13:15]

"For I know that my Redeemer lives, and He shall stand at last on the earth; and after my skin is destroyed, this I know, that in my flesh I shall see God." [Job 19:25-26]

Our testing, our trials, traumas and tragedies will always be for our benefit. However, when all the trials and troubles are over we find a higher purpose. When we walk through deep water, the outcome and benefits are for those who are to come. For God's own reasons He permits life-altering situations in our lives and the lives of our loved ones and acquaintances for His own glory.

*

This respite opens the door for the next chapter where we will see God's unfolding of angel hands to aid His children in this supernatural world.

Selah – Chapter Five

God's goodness and grace have been fleshed out in a single moment of time. A time of sacrificial horror designated as "Good Friday."

Is it for all the good that I have done? Is the good from those around me with boasts of glory? Or, perhaps it is because of all the good of combined humanity who serve or travel to foreign destinations to tell the story? Can it be the occasional fleeting sense to do what is best that makes me worthy of this monumental moment in time?

It is because of His goodness alone. A good lavished on all of us in blood covering victory. A gift purchased with deep and painful piercings by nails, thorns, spears and whip. Undeserving of the torment and pain He stood as man, a sacrifice, taking on Himself my iniquities, with lungs half-filled to rise and fall, grasping, for one more breath.

"And can it be that I should boast?"

There are vain things that have charmed me; extracting me from my first love. They have turned my head in directions not worthy, in the name of goodness, and right and even service.

"Were you there when they crucified my Lord?
Were you there when they crucified my Lord?
Oh, sometimes it causes me to tremble, tremble, tremble.
Were you there when they crucified my Lord?"*

*Traditional Spiritual

I was not there. Today I search my imagination, my intellect, and my mind to see what it must have been like. There is no comprehension or perspective that eludes me so as this, His goodness freely given on my behalf.

CHAPTER 6

"For He will command His angels concerning you to guard you in all your ways; they will lift you up in their hands, so that you will not strike your foot against the stone." v. 11 - 12

When reading this passage the promise of angelic protection is passed over or brushed aside by many of us without regard to the depth or potential consequence of such a promise. Who knows what God has chosen to do through the work of angels concerning our daily lives? Many disregard the work of angels as only a myth or something nice to think about, paint pictures of and possibly include in a song.

Peter Paul Rubens, the great Renaissance artist, painted angels as chubby infants with small wings. Angels have been painted as baby cherubs with harps in hand or tall blonde haired feminine beings in white robes. They are neither. If we were permitted eyes with which to see the spirit world, our lives would be forever changed. The supernatural is competent to deal with the supernatural. We are not equipped by our own intellect or personal skill set to battle that which we cannot see. Satan and his forces of dark angels are set out to wreak havoc on the human race. Therefore, we will find ourselves helpless if it were not for the assistance that God provides through the work of the Holy Spirit and the caring provision of His angels as they intervene on our behalf.

Psalm 103:20, "Bless the Lord, you His angels, who excel in strength, who do His word, heeding the voice of His word." The phrase, "His angels, who excel in strength" paints a realistic picture of these messengers of the Lord. II Chronicles 32:21 identifies the strength and power allotted to a single angel. "Then the Lord sent an angel who cut down every mighty man of valor, leader, and captain in the camp of the king of Assyria."

*

The Hebrew word for angel is *malach* and means messenger. Likewise, the Greek word is *angelos* also meaning messenger. On many occasions throughout scripture God used angels to deliver His message to His prophets and His people. Angels announced the birth of Samson, John the Baptist and Jesus. Charles Wesley poetically paints this picture of the Messianic announcement in his hymn, "Hark! The Herald Angels Sing."

> *Hark! The herald angels sing, "Glory to the new born King; peace on earth and mercy mild, god and sinners reconciled!" Joyful, all ye nations rise, join the triumph of the skies; with the angelic host proclaim, "Christ is born in Bethlehem!" Hark! The herald angels sing, "Glory to the new born King."*

An angel was sent to aid Abraham, Jacob, Daniel and Moses. Angels made a significant contribution to the Exodus experience of the Hebrew children, both in the forcing of Pharaoh to release them from captivity and in their forty years of wandering in the wilderness.

Many books could be written on the historical biblical exploits of angels in service to Jehovah God and to Jesus as the second person of the Trinity. In relation to our study in Psalm 91 and in particular verses 11 and 12, let us relook at how Satan used these verses in his second temptation of Christ, focusing on Matthew's gospel chapter 4 and verse 6. Satan initiated the conversation with, "He shall give His angels charge over you, and in their hands they shall bear you up, lest you dash your foot against the stone." Jesus did not fall prey to this abuse of scripture, just as He withstood the third temptation to worship Satan.

It is significant to conclude the temptations of Christ with Matthew 4:11. "Then the devil left Him, and behold, angels came and ministered to Him." "And behold," the fulfillment of Psalm 91 verses 11 and 12, "angels came and ministered to Him." Satan's abuse of this passage did not negate its fulfillment in God's perfect timing.

*

Identified by name in both the Old and the New Testament are both Michael and Gabriel. Scores if not hundreds and thousands of angels are referred to in scripture and only these two, along with Satan, are associated with specific names.

The holy angels of light worship God, are immortal, do not marry, are wise, obedient, and examples of meekness. Other references in scripture refer to them as mighty, holy, innumerable, and that they are not to be worshipped.

Let me clarify the application of this psalm by directing our attention to the service ministry of angels on our behalf. "Are they not all ministering spirits, sent out to render service for the sake of those who will inherit salvation?" [Hebrews 1:14]

Billy Graham wrote in his book **Angels**, "One of Satan's sly devices is to divert our minds from the help God offers us in our struggles against the forces of evil. However, the Bible testifies that God has provided assistance for us in our spiritual conflicts. We are not alone in this world! The Bible teaches us that God's Holy Spirit has been given to empower us and guide us. In addition, the Bible - in nearly three hundred different places – also teaches that God has countless angels at His command. Furthermore, God has commissioned these angels to aid His children in their struggles against Satan."

Scripture teaches in relation to Psalm 91:11-12 that angels minister to the righteous and act to "guard you in all your ways." There is no definitive teaching which states that we as His children have "guardian angels." However, scripture states the following:

"Take heed that you do not despise one of these little ones, for I say to you that in heaven their angels always see the face of My Father who is in heaven." [Matthew 18:10]

Genesis 24:7, "He shall send His angel before thee."

Genesis 24:40, "The Lord before whom I walk, will send His angel with thee, and prosper thy way."

Isaiah 63:9, "In all their affliction the angel of His presence saved them."

Acts 12:7, "And, behold, the angel of the Lord came upon him, and a light shone in the prison."

I do not intend to take these verses out of their original intended context. Rather, I am using them to validate that on occasion God used His angels to minister to His children. Still today angels are a vital link between God and man. They "rejoice over the repentance of even one sinner." [Luke 15:10] They are fascinated with watching the drama of salvation play itself out in the lives of individuals, as Peter beautifully describes in his first epistle chapter 1 and verse 12. "They were finally told that these things would not occur during their lifetime, (the lifetime of the prophets) but long years later, during yours. And now at last this Good News has been plainly announced to all of us. It was preached to us in power of the same heaven-sent Holy Spirit who spoke to them; and it is all so strange and wonderful that even the angels in heaven would give a great deal to know more about it." [TLB]

Angels do not do the work of the Holy Spirit; but, according to many references from God's Word they give protection and guidance as to the physical needs of man. They escort the saints in death as described in Luke 16:22. As a minister for more than forty years I can give many examples of the experiences of men and women who on their deathbed clearly identified angels in their rooms awaiting their passing. An example of an angel escorting saints into heaven is identified in Luke's gospel chapter 16 and verse 22. "So it was that the beggar died, and was carried by the angels to Abraham's bosom. The rich man died also and was buried."

*

With many possible references from which to draw I will conclude with Isaiah chapter 6 where God's messengers delivered His word to the prophet.

> In the year that King Uzziah died, I saw the Lord sitting on a throne, high and lifted up, and the train of His robe filled the temple. Above it stood Seraphim; each one having six wings: with two he covered his face, with two he covered his feet, and with two he flew. And one cried to another and said: *"Holy, holy, holy is the Lord of hosts; the whole earth is full of His glory!"* And the posts of the door were shaken by the voice of him who cried out, and the house was filled with smoke. So I said: "Woe is me, for I am undone! Because I am a man of unclean lips, and I dwell in the midst of a people of unclean lips; for my eyes have seen the King, the Lord of hosts."

Isaiah's vision takes us into the Lord's throne room and although we can only get a glimpse of what the prophet saw, there was clearly grandeur beyond description. The vision of the Lord, lifted high, with his robe sweeping to the floor both draping and filling the temple where multiple seraphim spoke in antiphonal chorus was overwhelming. What followed in the shaking of the door posts represents the awesome glory of God causing Isaiah to see his personal condition as well as the condition of his people.

"For He will command His angels concerning you," is aptly described in the Isaiah verse as well as Psalm 91. Angels protect, deliver from harm and bring God's message to us so that we may respond in obedience. Therefore we join the prophet with a similar response. "Because I am a man of unclean lips, and I dwell in the midst a people of unclean lips." [Isaiah 6:5] The cleansing from sin, as represented by the Seraphim taking the coal of fire from the altar and placing it on the unclean lips of the prophet, was preparatory for the question that was to follow. "Whom shall I send, and who will go for Us?" [Isaiah 6:8] The triune God is speaking of Himself, Jesus the Christ and the Holy Spirit, with the word "Us." Our response should echo that of the prophet, the disciples, missionaries and pastors who have answered this call through the centuries. "Here am I! Send me." [Isaiah 6:8]

*

Selah – Chapter Six

The hustle and bustle of non-rhythmic sounds had long subsided as twilight and mist collided not to be separated 'til morning. The sun was well hidden by the curvature of the earth and the dark was sparsely dotted with lights that made holes in night.

Yet, there was no comfort in knowing that a clean conscious makes for a soft pillow on this particular night. The heaviness of the world would hang as dead weight on shoulders not broad enough to bear it. Living in empathy for those who are hurting is difficult for many but especially those who want to fix it. Is it good that often we cannot fix it? Is it best for us to turn from ourselves and give up in despair?

The night was made for communion with an all-knowing and loving God - One who brings a peace that passes understanding; the same peace that cannot be imitated by the best of impersonators. The God of peace whispers words of comfort like "I will never leave you nor forsake you." Eyelids soon become heavy, and shoulders made tense by a day's struggles relax.

Soon the light of dawn will expel the black from door fronts and alleys. The hush of evening slowly turns into a morning's hum, which expands into non- rhythmic patterns. The bustle of morning leads to the anticipation of a new day.

"I will never leave you nor forsake you," [Hebrews 13:5] and "He will command His angels concerning you to guard you in all of your ways; they will lift you up in their hands, so that you will not strike your foot against a stone" brings rest to a heavy heart.

CHAPTER 7

"You will tread on the lion and the cobra; you will trample the great lion and the serpent." [v. 13]

Although this statement is metaphoric and presumes upon God for protection from all attacks, it might more clearly be understood in relation to attacks which could ultimately be deadly. The lion and the cobra were familiar foes to the ancients. Travelers had to be aware of both when on the road as they could become easy targets when making their way along narrow paths. The lion is powerful, fearless, and possesses great speed which makes his prey vulnerable while the cobra is filled with venom, leading to eminent death. Both were common in this arid country.

*

In taking a deeper look at this single verse one can easily see how the lion and the cobra, or serpent, possibly refer to Satan. Numerous verses from the Old and New Testaments identify Satan as one or the other.

First Peter 5:8 says, "Be sober, be vigilant; because your adversary the devil walks about like a roaring lion, seeking whom he may devour." This specific visual identifies a predator looking for the opportunity to overpower his victim. How does the enemy attempt to devour you and me who are heirs to the kingdom? The answer can be found in the Greek word for devil which means "slanderer." Therefore, he attacks his prey with lies, slurs, discouragement, and temptations identifying only the beginning of a much longer list of *flaming arrows.*

Jesus, fully God and fully man, found himself in midst of Satan's flaming arrows of temptation. Jesus referred to himself as the Son of Man over 80 times, and this was His preference in identifying who He was. So, being tempted in all ways like we are, Jesus the Son of Man entered the battle equipped with the *sword of the Spirit,* which is the Word of God. The use of scripture to combat the temptation concluded with Satan leaving. We are to use this same tool or weapon in our combat concerning the lies of hell delivered to us from the lion and the serpent. And like Jesus, we have the clear understanding that the war is not over, only this battle. "Now when the devil had ended every temptation, he departed from Him until an opportune time." [Luke 4:13 NKJV]

Genesis chapter three gives us our first glimpse of Satan as the deceiving serpent in the Garden of Eden. Paul makes reference to this same serpent when communicating to the church at Corinth, "But I fear, lest somehow, as the serpent deceived Eve by his craftiness, so your minds may be corrupted from the simplicity that is in Christ." [II Corinthians 11:3] It is therefore an objective of the enemy and his fallen band to corrupt the minds of Christ followers by polluting their thoughts with those things which bring dishonor to God. Those same thoughts lead to enslavement to fulfill the will of the captor.

Satan's ultimate demise and final defeat is stated in Revelation 12:9 where once again he is identified as a serpent. "So the great dragon was cast out, that *serpent* of old, called the Devil and Satan, who deceives the whole world; he was cast to the earth, and his angels were cast out with him." [NKJV] John the beloved disciple and author of this final book of the Bible are clearly definitive in his identity. As if in a paraphrase he was saying, "In case you don't know exactly who I am speaking of let me be clear. It is the great dragon, the serpent of old, the Devil and Satan."

The lion and serpent strike fear in their victim and intimidate all who walk casually down this spiritual path. The victim is often taken by surprise and therefore has neither time to retreat nor the time to draw his weapon to stand in battle. However, that is not the picture the psalmist paints in this verse. "You will tread on the lion and the cobra" is a portrait of confidence and courage, void of fear and timidity. "You will trample the great lion and the serpent" again portrays confidence which includes the finality of defeating the fearsome foe.

*

This is truly the picture of Christ's final accomplishment on the cross and His ultimate return that includes the death blow to not only Satan but his huge demon band, all of whom will be laid waste in the lake of fire. Paul writes to the Roman church,

"And the God of peace will crush Satan under your feet shortly." [Romans 16:20 NKJV] From the very beginning of Moses' writings in the Pentateuch we see this very prophecy initiated as God cursed the serpent in the garden stating, "So the Lord God said to the serpent: 'Because you have done this, you are cursed more than all cattle, and more than every beast of the field; on your belly you shall go, and you shall eat dust all the days of your life.'" [Genesis 3:14 NKJV] These words were a precursor to what He said next concerning the coming of Christ to rescue man from his now fallen state. These words were spoken, not to Satan manifest in the snake, but to Satan, the spiritual created being. "And I will put enmity between you and the woman, and between your seed and her Seed; He shall bruise your head, and you shall bruise His heel." [Genesis 3:15 NKJV]

Man, now in his fallen state, would need someone to deliver him from the death he would now ultimately face. The Seed referred to in this prophetic statement is the first reference of the coming Messiah. From Genesis to Malachi we will read prophecies of the one who would deliver man from his sin condition, redeeming a path to permanent dwelling with the Most High.

Therefore, we also are "more than conquerors." We are victors not through our own cunning, wisdom or strength, but "through Christ who gives us strength." It was Christ on our behalf who "disarmed principalities and powers, He made a public spectacle of them, triumphing over them in it." [Colossians 2:15 NKJV]

Respect is necessary when facing any enemy. Respect is not the same as fear. Fear is a tool the enemy uses against us to intimidate, like the roar of a lion, or spread of a cobra's head. Fear will not bring about victory. We have the privilege of stating a strong declaration of faith as did King David. "The Lord is my light and my salvation; whom shall I fear? The Lord is the strength of my life; of whom shall I be afraid." [Psalm 27:1]

*

Encouragement is purposeful in the writing of Psalm 91 and especially as the psalm crescendos to its peak in verse 13. Yet there are times when all of us will bow to the threats of the enemy and acquiesce to his dominance over us. Circumstances come that we have no control over, and we will waver in our confidence, though often behind a mask placed over a fallen countenance. It is then we wear a veil that once hid the evidence of standing in God's glory, and now that same veil covers the darkness of a waning faith.

The encouragement of the Almighty is continued in Christ's final words on the cross. It was on the cross where the final battle was waged and won on our behalf. That battle will never be fought again. These words of the God-man now resonate throughout the generations since the fall of Adam in the Garden to the final victory shout of a returning Redeemer, "It is finished."

*

Selah – Chapter Seven

Gratitude causes the countenance to shine and smooth wrinkles made deep by time. Such is seen on the beautiful face of a mother-to-be who carries, large bellied, a new life tucked inside, near a thankful heart. Moses' countenance had changed when he came down from the mountain with veiled face, thus hiding the manifest glory of God's presence. Veiled because of a future time when the glow would fade into a world of worry, anxious moments and the knowledge that some would scoff as if the radiance was fraudulent and meant only to keep them from their idols.

So, I plagiarize the Word of God in my heart and with my pen, knowing this same gratitude will brighten my countenance, smooth my wrinkled brow and remove the need for veil wearing.

John's vision in the Revelation identifies the glorified countenance of Christ, the Son of Man. "And His countenance was like the sun shining in its strength. And when I saw Him, I fell at His feet as dead. But He laid his right hand on me, saying to me, 'Do not be afraid; I am the First and the Last. I am He who lives, and was dead, and behold I am alive forevermore. Amen.'" [Revelation 1:16b – 18a NKJV]

CHAPTER 8

"Because he loves Me," says the Lord, *"I will rescue him; I will protect him for he acknowledges My Name."* v. 14

If we were to use the pronoun "I" multiple times consecutively in conversation it would appear to be braggadocios. However, with God it is a simple statement of fact because He is capable to do all He promises. God the Father is competent to fulfill this role and therefore has the privilege to communicate with authority, "I will take care of you." A good father would never allow an intruder into his home, and he would do whatever necessary to protect his family. The example of God the Father who tenderly watches over His children is further defined in the "I will" statements of verses 14-16.

> I will rescue him.
> I will protect him.
> I will answer him.
> I will be with him in trouble.
> I will deliver him.
> I will honor him.
> I will satisfy him with long life.
> I will show him My salvation.

*

These "I will" statements are promises ultimately fleshed out in the person of the Lord Jesus. They punctuate God's love for us as fulfilled on the cross. The American folk hymn, "*What Wondrous Love Is This*" as written in the beauty of Appalachian poetry reads:

> What wondrous love is this
> that caused the Lord of bliss
> to bear the dreadful curse for my soul.
> When I was sinking down
> beneath God's righteous frown,
> Christ laid aside His crown for my soul.

God's love was on display for the all the world to see that Good Friday, giving mankind a visual picture of God in the flesh-broken, beaten, and wounded. This scene has been recreated by painters, sculptors and writers for twenty centuries, and yet the renderings of these crucifixion scenes could never tell the full story of the horror on display. Christ suffering for a crime He did not commit would be impossible to capture on canvas or with stone.

"Behold what manner of love the Father has bestowed on us, that we should be called children of God!" [I John 3:1 NKJV]

The stipulation for God to do all He is promising in these concluding verses is found in the phrase "Because he loves me" or in the NKJV, "Because he has set his love upon Me." We will invest our time in this chapter on verse 14. As we begin this single verse study, we are reminded that "We love Him because He first loved us." [I John 4:19]

The word love in this setting means deep longing for God as one who has been on an extended trip and has desperately missed those to whom he is very close. This promise-heavy psalm no longer speaks in the third person. The change in tone not only personalizes the psalm but gives more depth to the relationship. Matthew Henry in his commentary states, "Some make this to be spoken to the angels as the reason of the charge given them concerning the saints, as if He said 'Take care of them for they are dear to me, and I have a tender concern for them.'" [*Matthew Henry's* Commentary, 482]

What is my responsibility or what am I to do in order to be the recipient of such tender care? This is truly an ancient question obviously pondered in the legalist mind of the Pharisees and worthy of consideration in our contemporary culture. We sense there must be a personal obligation on our part to merit this grace-filled love. The attempt is then made to pay this debt through good works or living a better life, thus proving ourselves worthy of this unmerited favor when in fact there is nothing we can do. Yet this truth evades us, producing new generations working to earn our rights with good deeds. Because of present and past failure, the tendency is to give up knowing we are incapable of living up to the high expectations we've set. The fatigue becomes overwhelming because everything tried in the past has failed us. Spiritual fatigue is the reason the key word **"rest"** found in verse one is so significant; our rest is a byproduct of us setting our love on Him.

*

God is in essence saying to his children, there is a key that opens the door to My fortress and the key is your love devotion to Me. If you are to dwell in My shelter and find rest you will enter by using this key.

The love relationship is damaged or broken when His children move their affections from Him to their idols. This broken relationship was seen in the wilderness experience of the Hebrew children when Moses' return was prolonged due to his speaking with God on Mount Sinai. The Hebrews constructed the golden calf to appease their sinful idol-worshipping nature. Often we too turn our affections from our Creator and construct idols to appease our sin nature. God did not share His glory in the story of the ungrateful wilderness tribe nor will He share it today.

Just as shade brings protection, it also brings comfort. For there to be shade there must be, as in this case, someone casting the shadow. A shadow does not appear without an object standing between the recipient of the shade and the light source. The shadow is cast by El-Shaddai, God Almighty. The light as identified here is a source of discomfort as one would feel from a hot and skin-burning sun during a summer afternoon. "He who dwells in the shelter of the Most High will rest in the shadow of the Almighty." [Verse 1]

Now, let us direct our attention to the two distinct promises in verse 14. The first promise is "I will rescue him." God is the speaker in this section identifying the blessing in store for those who love Him.

In many translations the word deliver is used in place of rescue. The transitive verb deliver means to set free as in the Lord's Prayer, "and lead us not into temptation but deliver us from evil." The assumption is we are being set free from captivity or saved from being taken captive.

God does not say, I will rescue him because he is without sin, kept all My commands, and therefore worthy to be delivered. The only precondition is our love for Him. Love does not necessarily stand alone in this setting of the psalm. Trust can be and often is an accompanying word in this love relationship and a major element in all relationships. I have heard and read numerous theologians state, "You cannot trust someone any further than you know them."

Trusting or having faith in God and His promises grows as we develop a more intimate relationship with Him through personal fellowship and personal experience.

*

Forty years ago, as I began my ministry, the Lord was gracious to allow this young green horn the privilege to go on staff in a mission-setting church in the Northern Plains of the United States. It was a terrific experience where numerical growth happened very quickly. One of my duties was to direct the church choir, and with my wife at the piano we joyfully began this journey. Moving from our native state of Texas in late August to this mountain wonderland was incredible, and by December our choir filled the existing choir loft and overflowed onto the stage where another row was added to seat the new additions. Often, members of the choir sat on the front pews and came onto the platform during the service to join the choir. There was much fulfillment accompanied with high expectations as the holiday season approached and our Christmas music was being prepared in celebration of Christ's birth. Choir robes were the standard attire during this era; yet, the continued additions in the choir eliminated the use of the inadequate number of robes hanging in the dressing rooms. However, everyone wanted to look their best for the coming special event. It was a Wednesday night and at the conclusion of rehearsal I was asked if we could purchase an extra thirty nine maroon choir robes and their white stoles which would give us exactly what we needed for all to have matching attire. I told the choir that new robes were not a priority for a growing church with many other needs, but we would ask the Lord if He would hear our simple request. Then we closed the rehearsal with prayer.

The next morning I was up early to catch a brief flight to Rapid City, South Dakota, where I was participating in a student ministry conference. After landing on a snow-covered runway, I exited the plane and was immediately met by a gentleman from Mississippi who asked me if I was part of the church student conference. After answering that I was, we began walking toward the baggage claim area together. Then he asked a most unforgettable question, a question I have revisited in my memory now for four decades. "Do you know of a church in need of some choir robes? Our church recently purchased new robes and so I am bringing these in hopes of finding a church in need." I quickly answered "Yes, I do. Our choir needs new robes."

He said, "I have them boxed up and they will be ready to return with you when you fly out tomorrow." After arriving home and unloading my suit case along with the extra boxes, I could not wait to tell my wife and then present them to the choir on Sunday morning. We quickly opened them in our living room to find not only our same maroon choir robes with the matching white stoles, but after counting there were, as you may have already guessed, thirty-nine. I still weep when reliving this story. The choir was exuberant and thanked the Lord many times. They looked and sounded spectacular that Christmas.

After these many years I consider God's love in this case on display in the provision of needed choir robes. I do not believe He provided the robes just to answer our prayer for additional robes. The provision was for us to see that we can trust Him in all things. Praying for choir robes would evolve into requests, such as, Lord how do I get through these days of chemo, or why did I lose my son at such a very young age. God's gracious gift of choir robes would be exchanged for His grace gifts yet to come.

The second promise is "I will protect him."

*

The word protect provides a broad-stroke use of the word from the original language and works perfectly well when translated into English. However, the phrase "set him on high" as used in the NKJV works just as well, with an additional picturesque and poetic flare. Depicted with the use of this phrase is a high inaccessible tower, a place far removed where one can escape for protection. If a man has escaped to the safety of a tower, we can assume two things. 1. He knows where the tower is located. 2. He has a way to get inside the tower. We do not attempt to access someone's residence unless we know the owner of the residence. Otherwise we are a thief or an intruder.

We know the tower is there because we are His children, and have access because we "know His name." Lord, it's me, your child, at your door. Knowing His name identifies that we are not foreigners or aliens looking for lodging, rather we are His children returning home.

"You shall hide them in the secret place of Your presence from the plots of man; You shall keep them secretly in a pavilion from the strife of tongues." [Psalm 31:20 NKJV]

*

Selah – Chapter Eight

How beautiful to hear, "I am Your own," as in a love song written in hopes of a lifelong commitment to oneness. You have made us your own through tender care, soft words and Your assurance of faithfulness. As Protector Provider You walk us through deep and dark waters - waters that rage and foam for our destruction and demise.

How quickly You have lifted us from the swelling current, as one would take a child into his arms hurrying him to the safety of a well-lit fortress. I often forget the price for my safe dwelling was paid centuries past - a blood-bought inheritance whose value can never be assessed.

CHAPTER 9

*

"He will call upon Me, and I will answer him; will be with him in trouble, I will deliver him and honor him." v. 15

The statement in the first half of this verse is straightforward and simple. He will answer us when we call upon Him. However in practice and application, it is not such a simplistic statement. The assumption is whenever we ask or call on Him, He is obligated to grant our request. Mary B. M. Duncan wrote in *Under the Shadow of the Almighty,* "I think we sometimes discourage ourselves by a misconception of the exact meaning of the expression, 'answer,' taking it to mean only grant. Now, an answer is not necessarily an acquiescence. It may be a refusal, an explanation, a promise or a conditional grant. It is, in fact, attention to our request expressed." [Spurgeon, *The Treasury of David*, 112]

The first presupposition is that there must be a question. Many times we assume that God simply understands that we have a need and therefore will provide for that need with no dialogue attached, and yet all intimate and personal relationships include good communication. James 4:2 and 3 states, "You do not have because you do not ask. You ask and do not receive, because you ask amiss, that you may spend it on your pleasures." [NKJV]

The writer of Hebrews proclaims, "Let us therefore come boldly to the throne of grace." This passage continues by stating, "That we may obtain mercy and find grace to help in time of need." [Hebrew 4:16 NKJV] In ancient times rulers expected all who entered their presence to enter with heads bowed in trepidation, as so many rulers were not approachable. Through the confident counsel of the Holy Spirit and the work of Christ, we find God is not only approachable, He is happy and pleased for us to enter His presence and have intimate fellowship with Him.

It is my practice to have a daily time alone with God, in a quiet secluded spot where I am not disturbed. This special time usually includes thanksgiving and praise, introspection, scripture reading and question asking. I conclude by meditating on a portion of scripture that I have just read and sit quietly to hear from God. How God speaks is significant and for me it is often through a verse of scripture. Many times the verse is one I've hidden away in my memory. These nuggets of Biblical truth have been stored for decades, and I am comforted by the reminder of scriptures often held since early childhood. Other times, I hear from God through the passage I have just read and still other times I hear a "still small voice" speaking clearly. I have noticed that God never speaks loudly, and therefore I must be quiet to hear. I sense that God is very present and cares deeply for me. I will often ask the Lord to confirm what I sense is from Him by giving me a "peace that passes understanding."

After many decades of practicing a time of quiet solitude it has been my experience that the deceiver, as the enemy of our souls cannot imitate or duplicate this God-given peace.

*

Yet God is not limited by the way He speaks to us. I am reminded of a story told to me by a young couple who were very good friends of my wife and myself. This couple was home on furlough after serving their first stint as missionaries to Africa where they worked as agricultural missionaries. Kenny had received a degree in agriculture from a Texas college, and along with his wife Patty, was impressed to provide knowledge of how to grow crops in some of the most desolate parts of the African continent. Knowing that provision of food and water would also offer opportunity to spread the gospel to a highly unreached people group, they worked tirelessly under very difficult circumstances. Their modest home was under armed guard each night by a local native armed with a four-foot blow gun and a hand full of poisoned darts. The distances traveled from village to village could take hours on unpaved and deeply rutted roads, and there was not the company of other missionary couples with which to fellowship on a routine basis. Much of Kenny's time was spent alone making his way to distant tribal villages.

He told me of one particular day when he left his small compound in the predawn darkness with only his sack lunch and a roughly-drawn map, knowing that it would be late evening or early morning of the next day before returning home. Kenny shared that during that morning drive he felt very alone and very small, wondering if what they were doing was making a significant difference in these remote settings. He said the sun's position in the sky told him it was approximately noon, so he pulled his vehicle over to the side of the road to eat what Patty had packed several hours earlier. While sitting on the side of the road with sandwich in hand he asked the Lord, "Do you even know that I am here?" He said the words had not completely come out of his mouth when at that very moment a native came out of the brush and crossed the road in front of him with nothing on but a t-shirt. Boldly written across the front of his t-shirt was the name of Kenny's high school alma mater. Kenny said, "I never again felt the need to ask that question."

"I will answer them before they even call me. While they are still talking with me about their needs, I will go ahead and answer their prayers." Isaiah 65:25 NLT

Pause and reflect on God's greatness and the depth of His blessing as you recount this young missionary's story.

Our personal mortality drives many of our questions. We can see today, and have a minimal perspective on the recent past, yet God sees yesterday, today and tomorrow. Because of this unique ability to see what lies ahead there is wisdom in placing our unseen future in His hands.

"...will be with him in trouble." Verse 15b

Much of this psalm is based around statements of protection. The writer of Psalm 91 directs us through the identification of God our protector who will stay the course with us in every possible situation and is our provision in times of need concerning fear, terror, death, and disaster. The psalmist clearly identifies throughout the psalm every possible need we may have and every situation in which we may find ourselves.

*

However, it is here in this brief six-word statement where we will most often find ourselves in our relationship experience with God. It is not a picture of God snatching us from the grips of terror and death or suddenly removing us from a dangerous situation, or of Him hiding us away in a protected fortress. The statement is He will be with us, and the impact of this statement is extraordinarily comforting. This is a very special promise of **His presence** with His saints as they find themselves in the middle of troubles. Many times, if not most times, God finds it best for His glory and our good to simply be with us.

Student pastors through the years have asked me this question when attempting to minister to students in crisis: "What do I say?" My answer is, "It is not necessary to say anything. It is more important to simply be there." Quick and shallow answers may come from a sincere heart but may not be helpful. We show we care by being there in their time of need.

*

The fifth of His seven final promises in this psalm is "I will deliver him and honor him." Verse 15

Psalm 91 is a song of deliverance from verse one in His provision of "shelter" through verse fourteen in His promise to "rescue." This is the first time the psalm speaks of honor. He gives honor to us, not because we have done anything to deserve such honor; rather it is a continued glimpse into His character as the loving Father bringing His heir near the throne. We know how good it feels to be honored by men, so consider how much greater the emotion to be honored by God, the Creator of all things? He honors us by calling us His children. He puts us in a place of honor at his table. He honors us by listening to our requests and being with us in trouble. He has honored us through the work of His Son on the cross, Who now has gone to prepare a place for us. This highest laurel wreath of honor has been placed on the heads of us who are His children.

*

סֶלָה

Selah – Chapter Nine

Come, ye sinners, poor and needy, weak and wounded, sick and sore; Jesus ready stands to save you, full of pity, love and power. Come, ye weary, heavy laden, lost and ruined by the fall; if you tarry till you're better, you will never come at all. I will arise and go to Jesus, He will embrace me in His arms; in the arms of my dear Savior, O there are ten thousand charms. *

Our sins are not cleansed as by a morning's dew, but fresh washed with an afternoon's shower left clean and white to sparkle in the light to come. You can believe in something you cannot see like the wind acknowledged by the bent of a tree.

*Come Ye Sinners, Poor and Needy. Words: Joseph Hart 1712 – 1768; Refrain, Anonymous. Music: Walker's Southern Harmony, 1835

CHAPTER 10

"With long life will I satisfy him and show him my salvation." v. 16

Long life is one of the final "I will" promises at the conclusion of this psalm. In the Old Testament the saint had a promise of long life because of obedience to the law such as found in Exodus 20:12. "Honor your father and your mother, that your days may be long upon the land which the Lord your God is giving you."

The promise of honor to us, His children, concludes verse fifteen. "I will deliver him and honor him." This same honor or respect is due to our parents and is punctuated with the same addendum of long life. Giving reverence to father and mother is a fulfillment of Old Testament law with special recognition on the part of the child to their authority over us, an authority that is accompanied by the responsibility to raise us up in the fear of the Lord and train us in the ways of righteousness for our protection, health, and peace.

*

Though almost nothing is known about the adolescent years of Jesus' life, there is a significant post in Luke 2:51-52. "Then He went down with them and came to Nazareth, and was subject to them, but His mother kept all these things in her heart. And Jesus increased in wisdom and stature, and in favor with God and men." Christ the God-man was "subject to them" is the key statement in the fulfillment of the Old Testament law "honor your father and your mother." The benefit of His subjection or obedience to his earthly parents was that "He increased in wisdom and stature, and in favor with God and men."

Solomon wrote, "My son, do not forget my law, but let your heart keep my commands; for length of days and long life and peace they will add to you." [Proverbs 3:1 and 2 NKJV] Lack of respect for the law propagates juvenile delinquency, and many times this attitude of disrespect shortens life as a natural byproduct of that lifestyle.

The nineteenth century American theologian Albert Barnes wrote, "The margin here is 'length of days;' that is days lengthened out or multiplied. The meaning is I will give him length of days as he desires, or until he is satisfied with life." [Spurgeon, *The Treasury of David*, 113 (taken from *Barnes' Notes on the Whole Bible*)] Key in his exposition of this verse is the word "satisfy." This is a life not only filled with days but rather a fully satisfying life which has had purpose and meaning. Many have lived long lives that end without the satisfaction of contribution as invested in others, while others live briefer yet completed lives through their works for the kingdom, causes of evangelism and missions, and their personal ministry in the lives of people.

*

To the Hebrew nation, living a long fulfilled life was considered a blessing as one lived long enough to see the birth of their children, their grandchildren and their grandchildren's children. We see this example stated at the culmination of Abraham's life, "Then Abraham breathed his last and died in a good old age, an old man full of years, and was gathered to his people." [Genesis 25:8 NKJV] It is significant to focus on the words *good* and *full* in this descriptive conclusion to the father of the Jewish nation. Implied is that Abraham lived a fully satisfied life by way of the same promise now made available to all who dwell in the *shelter of the Most High.*

"Oh, satisfy us early with Your mercy, that we may rejoice and be glad all our days!" [Psalm 90:14 NKJV]

The perfect conclusion to Psalm 91 is as written, "show him My salvation." [Psalm 91:16] And now the God who has been providing, saving, protecting, covering, delivering, rescuing, honoring and satisfying brings it to a close with this word, I will now "show." What more would anyone want from such a gracious, loving Father than to see His finished work as gifted to us?

Paul places an exclamation point with this same thought when writing to the church at Ephesus. "But God who is rich in mercy, because of His great love with which He loved us, even when we were dead in trespasses, made us alive together in the heavenly places in Christ Jesus, that in the ages to come He might show the exceeding riches of His grace in His kindness toward us in Christ Jesus." [Ephesians 2:4-7 NKJV]

John MacArthur in his Study Bible Notes on this verse wrote, "Salvation, of course, is very much for the believer's blessing, but it is even more for the purpose of eternally glorifying God for bestowing on believers His endless and limitless grace and kindness. The whole of heaven glorifies Him for what He has done in saving sinners." [*The MacArthur Study Bible*, (Nashville: Thomas Nelson Inc., 1997), 1805]

As we have rested and resided in the dwelling of the Most High, now we are made a "dwelling" as His church for the third person of the Trinity, God's Holy Spirit. "In whom you also are being built together for a dwelling place of God in the Spirit." [Ephesians 2:22 NKJV]

Adam was given protection and provision, as was Abraham, the father of a lineage that could not be numbered. Joseph after being sold into Egyptian slavery by his brothers ultimately provided for these same brothers during time of famine; and Moses, the deliverer of the Hebrew children, experienced God's rescuing hand when pursued by Pharaoh's army. Verse after verse and chapter after chapter of the Old Testament tells stories of God saving His people from calamity due to His righteousness, mercy and grace.

To save means to deliver or rescue from peril. In concluding this psalm with the words "show him My salvation," we are reminded of everything that has proceeded these final words of blessing and encouragement, with the understanding that the troubles that have plagued and followed us are now forever far behind us.

*

The song written by the sons of Korah, Psalm 46, is a reminder of all that we have read, studied and now hidden away in our hearts.

> God is our refuge and strength, a very present help in trouble. Therefore we will not fear, even though the earth be removed, and though the mountains be carried into the midst of the sea; though the waters roar and be troubled, though the mountains shake with its swelling, there is a river whose streams make glad the city of God, the holy place of the tabernacle of the Most High. God is in the midst of her, she shall not be moved; God shall help her just at the break of dawn." [Vs. 1-5] "... Be still and know that I am God; I will be exalted among the nations, I will be exalted in all the earth! The Lord of hosts is with us; the God of Jacob is our refuge. [Vs. 10-11 NKJV]

As we now fast forward a few thousand years to the present, we are immediately ready to raise the question, "Are these promises available to us today?" The answer of course is yes, as God never changes, and "is the same yesterday, today and forever." [Hebrews 13:8 NKJV] Jesus has fulfilled the legacy of His Father by coming as the perfect, unblemished sacrificial lamb, fit and competent to take away the sins of the world. The God of Adam and Abraham keeps giving gifts to all who will receive this ultimate sacrifice of His only Son, as sufficient to take care of their own sin debt.

As God gives comfort through the writing of Psalm 91 to all who would read it and choose to enter His fortress refuge, so

Christ comforts first His disciples and now us with these words. "Let not your heart be troubled; you believe in God, believe also in Me. In My Father's house are many mansions (*dwelling places*); if it were not so, I would have told you. I go and prepare a place for you. And if I go and prepare a place for you, I will come again and receive you unto Myself; that where I am, there you may be also. And where I go you know, and the way you know." [John 14:1-4 NKJV]

✲

Selah – Chapter Ten

Today I will hang my instrument on the bent tree by the river where it will pick up the sounds and the rhythms of the moving waters. The bird will interrupt with his song along with the tympani roll of the occasional beast. Legato phrases transpose to new melodies as they splash against the ancient rocks worn smooth by their own suffering. Though the seasons will age my instrument the song will be replayed to its Creator Composer in times of reflection, as there is no song as beautiful as the endless symphony He writes.

Often I wonder, is this song only for my ears to hear and my soul to bear? If so, let me listen now lest the years cause me to go deaf and the song vanishes so I can no longer recall the harmonies that once raised me to the heights. Raise my soul again, if only as a brief interlude to a greater finale.

GUIDELINES FOR SMALL GROUP LEADERS

All study of scripture is relevant for the student of God's Word. Historical accounts, prose, songs, prophecy, and the New Testament all lend themselves to life changing application for the one who would choose to dig deep into this sacred literature. A good student of the Word will read for understanding so that information can be retained. The natural flow will be three-fold: observing what is being said in scripture, interpreting the section of scripture in context to the chapter, and then applying what you've read to your personal life make up the three-fold flow. The student who takes the time for personal application will discover the opportunity to share the learned truth with others.

If you are using _Rest in the Shadow_ as a small group Bible study here are some suggestions as to how you can make each session a success. Each chapter is designed as a forty-five to sixty minute study. Following the simple guidelines below will help equip you to lead your small group Bible study.

Preparation

1. Read the chapter ahead of time and make notes as to how these select verses of scripture apply to your life.

2. Follow the directions for *Bible Study Questions* found in the next section.

3. It is often helpful to use a good Bible commentary either found in a Study Bible or from a good bookstore. Many excellent commentaries exist for every book of the Bible.

4. Watch the clock so as not to get distracted or "chase rabbits" as this can hinder future small group study times. Guide the class to stay on task.

5. Always start on time and have someone in the small group lead in prayer asking God to give insight to best understand the passages of scripture for that day.

6. Though my personal stories as author may be helpful, please feel free to use your own experiences or those from one of your group members. A real life story helps validate what is being taught, allowing participatory involvement in the scriptural application.

7. Small groups work best when class interaction and participation are encouraged. The study is not a lecture but a format for presenting truth for personal discussion and application.

8. Introductory questions asked early in the study will help guide the class to see the theme of each week's scripture passage.

BIBLE STUDY GUIDELINES

Here are some helpful tips in order to have a successful Bible study.

1. Use the questions exactly as written and occasionally restate the question in your own words.

2. It is never wrong to have a time of silence as the participants will often need time to digest the question in order to give a thoughtful answer.

3. Do not answer the questions yourself, as the leader, as this often leads to a feeling that any other answer may be incorrect. Repeat the question slowly in order to give more time to think about what is being asked. Allow the class to answer the questions.

4. Never just stop with a single answer. Rather, ask "What other answers do you have?" Several in the group should have time to respond.

5. Do not react negatively to an answer. Be encouraging and include others even if the answer is off task. Use questions

like, "What do you think about that answer?" or "Does someone have another take on this question?"

6. Let the conversations stimulate other responses. I have used the following statement at the beginning of many studies. "We do not have arguments during our Bible study. We only have dialogue." Many times it is appropriate to simply move on.

7. It will be beneficial to summarize what has been said or taught during or at the conclusion of each study.

8. Conclude in prayer asking God to use His Word to make life change for those who have participated in that night's study of scripture.

CHAPTER ONE
BIBLE STUDY QUESTIONS

An * is inserted throughout each chapter to designate that a question can be asked at this point. The questions are in order as to when and where they are to be presented.

Chapter One

*What does the title <u>Rest in the Shadow</u> infer as we prepare for this study of Psalm 91? Why do you think this? Does God's presence give you a sense of peace? Why or why not?

*On what occasions would you need a place of refuge? What would this place look like to you and why?

*What are some things that would keep us from living in the dwelling described in these first verses of this Psalm? Discuss these answers individually and identify why they are valid or invalid.

*Do the fears of the unknown cripple you from trusting God? Why does fear stand in the way of our relationship with God?

CHAPTER TWO
BIBLE STUDY QUESTIONS

*Have you ever felt trapped in a bad situation that you had no control over or had not expected? How did it make you feel? Was there an easy way of escape?

*Since many things that look attractive and promising may be alluring, what are some guidelines that you can use to keep from being snared? Are there ways to identify the artificial bait and the real thing? How helpful would it be to recognize what is real and what is artificial?

*God's deliverance from a catastrophe is an act of grace. What acts of grace has God performed on your behalf? Did you recognize it was God at work? When did you come to the realization that God had done a work on your behalf and saved you from a very bad situation?

*List some things that bring you comfort. Are we responsible, as children of God, to offer comfort to others who may need rescuing? What might this look like, or how might this action be fleshed out?

*What can you conclude about the personality of God after participating in this study? What makes God trustworthy in all situations of life?

CHAPTER THREE
BIBLE STUDY QUESTIONS

*Have you ever been in a fearful situation where you had no recourse or way out? How did that feel? Have you ever been rescued from a difficult event? Is God's promise comforting as stated in verses 5 through 8? Why or why not?

*Often danger comes from lies and accusations and not physical harm. How are we to handle lies and accusations that are designed to hurt or destroy us? Since "we are not battling against flesh and blood," what is our source of strength and protection?

*Have you been struck with a pestilence that comes out of nowhere, does its damage, and then leaves? Was there fear attached to the damage of the pestilence? When the scripture says, "You will not fear," how is that possible? How do you or we detach fear from such an event?

*Are there times when God provides protection for His children and they never know about it? Does Hebrews 13:5b, "I will never leave you nor forsake you," relate to the verses in Psalm 91:5-8? How?

*What are some ways you can use the difficult events of your life to minister to others facing similar problems?

CHAPTER FOUR
BIBLE STUDY QUESTIONS

*Do you often wonder why the wicked seem to prosper and others who are moral seem to struggle? Why does God allow this to happen, even if it is only for a season?

*The blood that was painted over the door posts of the Hebrews who were enslaved in Egypt gave them protection. This blood was a foreshadowing of something yet to come. What was to come? Are there other Old Testament examples that you can name?

*Since safety comes from our "trust in the Lord," then why do we find ourselves in peril and trouble on so many occasions? Is the phrase "trust in the Lord" only a cliché, or is there a deeper understanding of trust that we need to grasp?

*What are some ways we can "make the Most High" our dwelling? List them.

*God does not keep us from evils such as terror, the arrow, the pestilence and the plague; rather, He keeps us from the fear of evil. Is there comfort in knowing this truth? Why or why not?

CHAPTER FIVE
BIBLE STUDY QUESTIONS

*Do you feel angels are still about the business of doing the things God designed them to do, or are they only Old Testament beings who no longer have relevance?

*Since God's Word is our only weapon against the enemy, how do we use it in spiritual battle? What are some examples of the "flaming arrows" of the enemy? What part does recognition of our enemy play in this battle?

*How are we able to "strengthen the brethren" after we've survived trials, trauma, or troubles? Do you have some examples to share? Why would sharing your own story be beneficial to others?

*Since the real life situations that we will all walk through are for His glory and our benefit, does it make it easier while in the middle of the struggle? Should it make it easier? Will today's study of God's Word prepare you for the unseen things that you will face in the future?

CHAPTER SIX
BIBLE STUDY QUESTIONS

*Since God can and has worked on our behalf by His own hand and through the work of His angels, what role do we have in His plan for our future? Are we observers or participants or both?

*Though Satan used scripture in tempting Jesus, it was misuse of scripture. Are there others who misuse or proof text scripture to prove their point or manipulate to get what they want? Do you know of examples? How have they manipulated God's Word to make it fit their needs?

*God made the magnificent creation of angels to do His work and bring Himself glory. Why do we spend little or no time in recognizing angels as God's messengers and on many occasions as instruments to aid man?

*Should the existence of angels direct us to a loving God or to the worship of angels? Why or why not? Since all of God's creation is designed for His own glory, how should we see ourselves and the messenger angels He has created?

CHAPTER SEVEN
BIBLE STUDY QUESTIONS

*We will all succumb to death. Some earlier and some later, but life's conclusion is the same for all men. However, God will on occasion protect us from untimely death and the one who would be the instrument of such a death. What are some ways He will protect us? What might our part be in this protection?

*An intimidated prey is always more vulnerable. With that in mind, what will cause you and me to be less intimidated by a foe? How can we use this to our advantage when battling this opponent?

*Knowing that Christ has won the battle and is the one who gives us our strength, what are practical ways to put this relationship to use in our conflicts? When we do things in our own strength, what is the outcome? What is the lesson learned through these experiences?

*What is the encouragement to us as children of God in Christ's final words, "It is finished." As these words, "It is finished," ring loudly in our ears, are they comforting and helpful?

CHAPTER EIGHT
BIBLE STUDY QUESTIONS

*God's *I will* promises as found at the conclusion of Psalm 91:14-16 show His deep love for us. Take a moment and contrast God's *I will* promises with the Isaiah 14:12-15 *I will* statements. Who do you wish to serve? Why?

*Why do I feel as if we must do something to earn God's love? Are there things in scripture that direct us to a works based relationship?

*What are possible scenarios in which we may find ourselves so that we need to be rescued? What does it feel like to be rescued from a bad situation, event or calamity? What role does gratitude play for the one being rescued? How do we show gratitude?

*Who is responsible to protect others close to them? List who they are and why they are responsible. Why does God, in the role of Father, offer us protection?

*It is obvious that we as dwellers in the shelter of the Most High will find protection. Are there events that may occur that will remove us from this source of protection?

CHAPTER NINE
BIBLE STUDY QUESTIONS

*Is God obligated to answer our requests and be in a position to save us from every hurtful or harmful experience? Why or why not?

*Do you often get disappointed when God does not immediately answer your requests? Do you get disappointed when God answers your request but not in the way you had hoped? What should be your response?

*Why do we most often find ourselves in trouble? Since most trouble comes from our bad choices, should we expect God to snatch us out of the situation? Why or why not?

*What is the sense you have when people gather 'round you in support when you are hurting? Does it feel good just to have their company? God's promise to "be with us" should bring comfort and peace. Has this been the case in your personal struggles?

*Have you ever received a special honor or recognition? Does that same sense occur when you are recognized as a Christ follower?

CHAPTER TEN
BIBLE STUDY QUESTIONS

*Is long life always a blessing? What is the significance of long life as it relates to the final verse of Psalm 91?

*What would make for a satisfying life? Make a list. What would be on the list of a believer who has faithfully followed, placed his love on, and dwelt with a loving God? How similar are these lists?

*What does salvation look like to you? How would you describe the emotion of being shown salvation at the conclusion of your life? Would this alter your present decisions and attitude about life?

*As this study of Psalm 91 is concluded, what are some things you will take away from it? Is this Psalm applicable today? How so? Do you sense there will be life change after investing these ten weeks in this study of Psalm 91? How will this change take place?

64676804R00066